The Many Leaves of Wisdom

ISBN-13: 978-0-9846347-0-5
ISBN-10: 0-9846347-0-3

First Printing, February, 2011

Cover design by ThomasMax

Cover picture by James Browne

Back cover photo of Mr. Schaible by Nicole Cordisco

Graphic Design Assistants: Sarah Washington, Chris Faulkner

Published by:

ThomasMax Publishing
P.O. Box 250054
Atlanta, GA 30325
404-794-6588
www.thomasmax.com

The Many Leaves of Wisdom

Trevor Schaible

ThomasMax

Your Publisher
For The 21st Century

This book is dedicated to my grandmom Grace (1916-2003)

who blessed me with her wisdom and kindness;

to my mother Joy

for her caring inspiration and humor

when I was a child and still to this day,

and for my father Milt (1940-2009)

for his strength and also for setting me up

with the hanging bamboo basket chair

for my campsite in the woods behind our house,

of which I`ll never forget.

INTRODUCTION

From the time when I was a child I always loved the forest. Being quite shy, it was my place of refuge. I reveled in the solitude of nature and came to know a peace within myself amidst the trees. If I was ever troubled, there is where I would find my grounding. Before I ever knew of meditation, the woods would bring me to that place inside.

The changing seasons, and also leaves, are to me a reflection of our own lives and our transformations. The winds and weather are as our moods. The imagery of each season in all their many colours play a large role in influencing my poetry. Sometimes the realm of fantasy, spirituality and dreams as well. For the creatures of the Earth, the innocent ones who cannot speak for themselves, I try to add my voice for their protection and treatment with compassion.

It is my intention with this, my book of poetry, to hopefully bring to you some measure of peace and love within and also for the wondrous environment surrounding us. May your Sacred Path be filled with enchantment and grace, and your own Life's Mysteries be blessed, forevermore.

~Trevor L Schaible

Black Poplar

Pounding Soul

Away I fly to farther skies
Destroying my hunger and heightening my eyes
For now the star is about to rise
With my pounding soul amidst dark demise

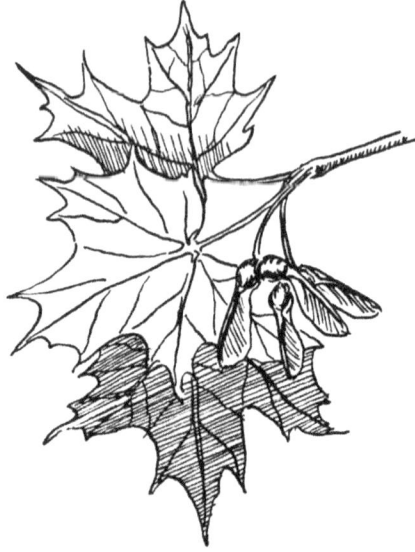

Sugar Maple

Autumns' Grace

I walk down paths
Amongst the trees
With my companion
The autumn breeze

She guides me softly
Far away
Into a meadow
And here we stay

She shares her song
So joyfully
Within her voice
She sings to me

She shows me beauty
With graceful ease
Enriched in colours
Her wind-swept leaves

Shell-bark Hickory

Nevermore

May the rain come down
In mighty swells
To strike the ground
And ring like bells

For such this sound
With crushing thunder
Descending lightning
To rend asunder

And such a torrent
Tormented winds
To sweep away
These unclean sins

So scour the land
Of all not pure
These blackened skies
Of nevermore.....

Alder

The Breath of Leaves

The mighty winds
Caress the trees
And ever softer
The gentle breeze

To soothe our souls
With playful tease
They spawn such pleasure
The breath of leaves

Silver Maple

Journey for the Unicorn

Amidst the ancient forests
Enchanted by the wild
Where nature spreads her flowered wings
So soon was I beguiled

My journey for the unicorn
To seek her fabled powers
The healing she could then provide
Within these forests' towers

A voice among the treetops
Now floats upon the breeze
While gentle whispers guide my pathway
And direction now I seize

A stream lies before me
With the water clear as day
And the current now I follow
To a waterfall at play

Colours flow before me
As a rainbow mist now flies
Descending to the unicorn
This graceful creatures' eyes

Mine own shine to her feelings
And shared a moments' face
With smiles sweet upon our souls
We mentally embrace

Trevor L. Schaible

Big Leaf Magnolia

Mother Emotions

I lay here as I'm mesmerized
Tickled by her tones
She whispers her sweet harmony
While soft wind gently moans

A flowering burst of raindrops
Now cleanses soul and skin
Descending as a leaf descends
As thoughts of past begin

Scarlet Oak

The Many Leaves of Wisdom

Inside this book I call my lifetime
With tales both great and small
Reflections of the mystery
Which rest within us all

Upon this Earth I've traveled
With kindness and with grace
While smiling the Sunshine
So pure upon my face

These many leaves of wisdom
Descending from above
The knowledge of my friendships
The colours of my loves

In the twilight skies of autumn
With my dreams both past and new
I've all my wishes brightened
By these memories of you

Pine Oak

Treetop Songs

All throughout the forest
There's a tale that shall be told
Within the midst of treetops
Hear their whispers young and old

As the wind portrays their feelings
And they're tossed from side to side
They all grasp others branches
With their wisdom they can guide

Their roots are tunneled deeply
In the ground they find their home
So warmth is gathered carefully
Inside the woodland dome

Water is their bloodstream
And the Earth is Mother's womb
They breathe to us their sweetened air
To destroy them means our doom.

Western Bottle-Brush Grass

Windsong

As chimes sing for the windsong
A breeze now speaks to me
It tells of Life's adventures
And allows me now to see

This time we're in is mass confusion
Questioning this day
But I shall wait for those few times
When minds and souls shall play

Fraser Magnolia

Pure Reality

It is light in the woods
At nighttime and in in day
A peaceful sanctuary
With everything at play

It's brighter on the shore
With Sun and Moon at sea
A soft wave gently whispers
Of pure reality

Eastern Hophornbeam

The Dawn of Soulmates

Come to me, my soulmate
Just like the time before
When once you journeyed
Upon the waves of a sacred dream
Draped in your garment transparent
Yet still containing mysteries
Bringing harmony with your deepest eyes of knowledge
Revealing in their wisdom a path to find you again
Through the forest of such warmth and beauty
The place where our spirits joined for the first incredible moment
And the promise upon your lips
Your voice the song of sweetest remembrance

The enchantment of your smile

Dance with me as like two leaves
Grown from the same branch of a brightly shining tree
Intertwined and in flight
Spiraling with the wind
As we turn and rise we persevere
Seeking a place to rest our coloured souls
Together, forever
Creating patterns on tapestries of love
Always to see the setting of the sun
The ascension of the moon
While in the day to bathe in the light
Of the wondrous possibilities
Beginning in the mists of mornings' dawn

American Beech

Life and Death

Upon one mountain life
On the other now lies death
A battle waiting in a void
With but a lonely breath

To choose which side to stand for
If I should dare at all
I'll breathe into myself this life
For I know that death shall fall

Cat Greenbrier

Frolic

Deep within the forest
There is magic to be found
With mystery in the leaves
Enchantment all around

While all throughout the day
And ever through the night
The frolicking of creatures
Brings merriment to light

Bristly Buttercup

Swirl

I sit and brood, an ugly mood
So deep within my thoughts
And as this does continue
So chaos shall be wrought

A spiraling of emotions
Cascading psychic drain
They swirl like such tornadic winds
To cycle once again

Shining Willow

Shining Soul

My eyes shall fade
As will my flesh
But not within
My spirits depth

For while this time
'Dost taketh me
My shining soul
Forever free

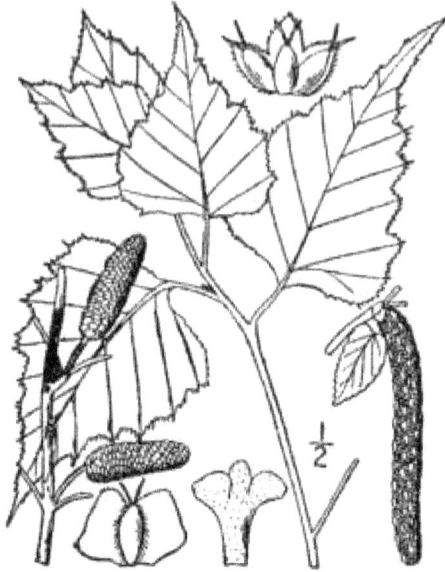

Gray Birch

Leaves of the Breeze

I catch a leaf upon the wind
Descending through the sky
Falling from the Tree of Life
To touch the ground and die

Before it's splendour turns to dust
Its eyes now gently fly
To give out one last final wish
And sadly so do I.

Black Raspberry

Sparkling Sun

As the sun shall rise
With orange glow
Creating colours
From mists below

Its light shall come
In sparkling array
Creating wonders
To begin each day

Kelsey's Locust

Thoughts

Staring through the leaves of trees
At stars adorning them
Like twinkling decorations
With a touch of dawn
Rising over the horizon
Bringing colour to this mornings thoughts

So inspirational this background
Giving me memories of times of past
Reflections like the glittering mist
As the sun creates an array of rainbows
Refractions of splendour
Which only I, right here, right now can see....

I revel in nature's wonder....

In the constancy so glorious
I'm captured by the endless possibilities
Arising with each new day
The cycles returning and spiraling
Like rhymes of verse
Poetic and structured
Yet each one exciting and mysterious
In their very own special ways...

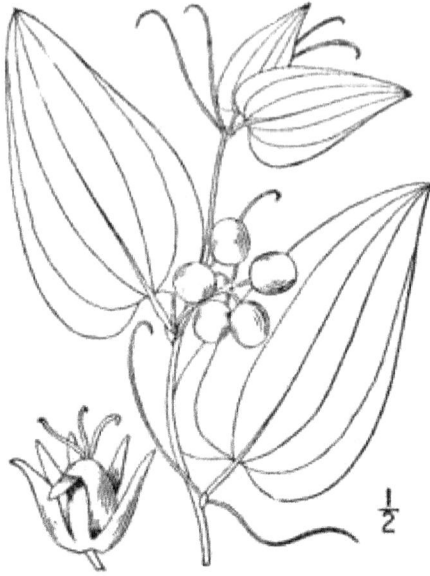

Coral Greenbrier

The Sounding Stream

I journey up a mountain
Through densely wooded forest
In search of pixie rose quartz
Adventure at its purest

But elusive is the pathway
Thought I've been here once before.
The trail is now forgotten
As I seek the stones' allure

A moment now I pause
For something do I sense
A calling of the eldritch kind
To it's source I now commence

As I make my way, beguiled
A stream-sound fill my ears
It guides me to the crystals
And then it disappears

Enfolding warmth spreads through me
As I gather up my prize
Reflecting on life's mysteries
Unboundless as the skies

Mexican Morning Glory

Smile in a Mirror

Smile in a mirror
As you look into your eyes
And tell yourself "I love you"
There's nothing to despise

Yes, smile in a mirror
With every passing glance
Just as a quick reminder
For sure your soul will dance

But if there is no mirror
And one is not around
Picture your reflection
And smiles shall be found

So smile in a mirror
Allow your sun to shine
The dawn will rise within you
And happiness you'll find

Smooth Ticktrefoil

Dancing Soul

In every gesture
In every breath
I feel this nature
Her sweet caress

In every season
In every leaf
Revealed its spirit
So deep beneath

For when I gaze
Amongst the trees
I see myself
My inner breeze

And when there's dancing
As with the feather
My soul is lifted
Amidst fine weather

Trevor L. Schaible

Spotted Touch-Me-Not

Innocence Cries

I hear the cries of animals
Pleading for their lives
Unknowing in their innocence
Of why they are to die

They're born into this chaos
To only know defeat
Tortured at the slaughterhouse
Providing someones' meat

Unspeakable their agony
In labs of vivisection
Or cast aside and sent off
For a science class dissection

And then there is the circus
Who beat them to compliance
With babies torn from mother's love
Who are killed for their defiance

Jaws of steel entrap them
Or raised just for their fur
Their skin ripped off while conscious
Man's vanity impure

We should be their sworn protectors
From this universal madness
As they look to us with weeping eyes
From this, their world of sadness

Cypress

Lullaby's Tale

Here is but a story
A lullaby of reasons
The tale of why I love you
In all your changing seasons

Just like the forests' branches
As they reach toward the sun
Forever this connection
Thus binding us as one

And like the oceans water
Enchanted misty veils
Their moonlit tides I journey
To your shores I set my sails

For as the winds they guide me
With storms and gentle breeze
I'm drawn into your wondrous eyes
Their soul-deep ancient seas

Fremont's goosefoot

Secret Breeze of Colour

Secret breeze of colour
Felt by no-one else but I
Brush lightly, soft, across my face
Enchanted by the sky

The greenish hue of Springtime
As Winter slowly dies
This changing transformation
Reflects now in my eyes

Beach Plum

The Paradise Path

I walk through paths of honeysuckle
With dawn carnelian skies
Surrounded by the wondrous scent
As beauty fills my eyes

I breathe in deep this paradise
As thoughts of love begin
For now and for forever
This journey lies within

Bear Oak

The Hollow Tree

I met a tree
Amongst the wood
Though hollowed self
So strong it stood

The wind did crack
My brittle skin
So cold outside
I stepped within

Inside this shelter
I heard a sound
A dream-like whispering
Concealed around

It spoke of times
In days of young
When Earth was pure
And forests sung

The songs of olde
All words foregone
Now tales and myths
For trees to spawn

This being in pain
Now heals my own
Its shade from winter
Becomes my home

Smallflower Pawpaw

The Healing Waves of Harmony

The energy of cosmos
It follows me around
Reflections in a moonstone
Where spirals can be found

For as the suns' carnelian
And oceans' lapis blue
Bring healing waves of harmony
I send them all to you

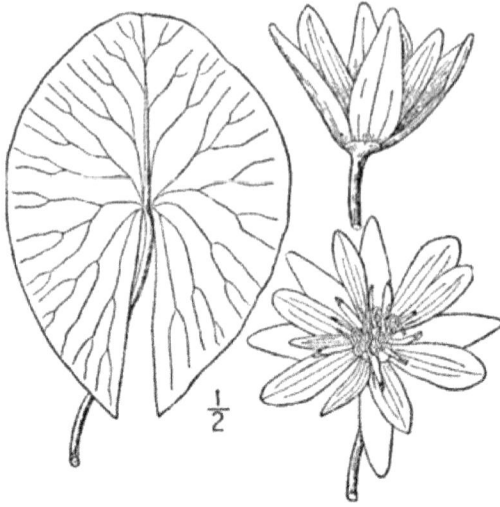

$\frac{1}{2}$

Pygmy Waterlily

With Grace

So mighty sound of rushing water
What will you say today?
Your currents flowing through my thoughts
Bring tastes of yesterday

Oh leaf, you fly on spiral winds
Please dance yourself to me
And grant me wishes with your love
I'll catch you happily

To ocean I give back to you
A crystal pure and clear
To cleanse your constant splashing waves
With harmony for years

And last the sky, but first with dawn
You grace the Earth with sun
With this creating coloured visions
Enlightening us as one.

Small Greenbrier

Songs of the Valley Wood

I lay amidst a flower bed
Amongst the valley wood
The sun sends chills of harmony
My senses, understood

I capture winds of natures' songs
The 'feather sing at day
For now I learn to persevere
And let them be their way

Balsa

The Many Sands of Friendship

I speak to you by day
You honour me at night
While answering my questions
These mysteries at flight

For far across the waters
You dwell in different lands
But time stands not between us
This friendships many sands

Ashleaf Maple

Spiritual Embrace

Your embrace can calm the ocean
Your touch could charge the sky
Your eyes divine, the deepest soul
And capture such as I

Your scent the sweetest flower
Like blossoms in the field
Your spirit soars on gentle winds
As beauty now revealed

Swamp White Oak

Amidst Rainbow Leaves

As Autumn comes
And change begins
With wind-swept rain
On shifting winds

Caress my soul
Within the breeze
While lifting and dancing
Amidst rainbow leaves

Cockspur Hawthorn

You and Eye

I feel as if I'm with your mind
Watching through your eyes

Seeing wonders sought, you find
Knowing you are wise

For all the tears inside your soul
With everyone who dies

And all the love which evil stole
Together we shall rise

Red Maple

The Dance of the Falling leaves

And so within a breath they fly
The dance of the falling leaves
So guided now by natures' eyes
They're welcomed by the breeze

For all their lives they have grown
Awaiting now this day
And all the wisdom they have known
Shall never fade away.

American Chestnut

Etchings

Etchings carved, and etchings drawn
Remembering the past of old dawn
The battles fought and battles won
Upon my sword, not be undone

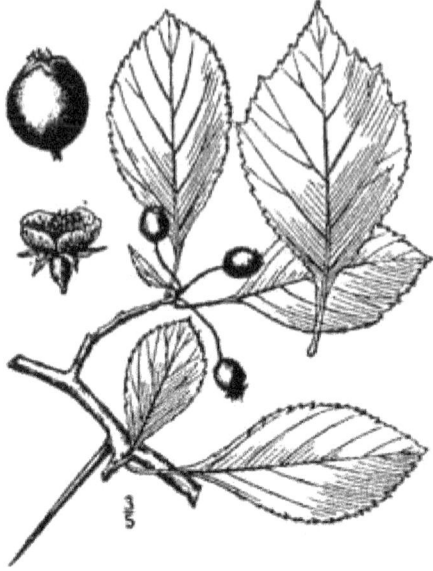

Bush Hawthorne

Intentions

A deep emotional being
For this is what you'll see
Inside these depths a wellspring
Of such vitality

With visions of forever
I persevere each day
While gathering such wisdom
Experienced my way

Expressions of my feelings
Contained within these eyes
Their radiance like star shine
So brightening the skies

A love, revealed to all
Projected my reflections
For this shall be my swansong
My greatest of intentions

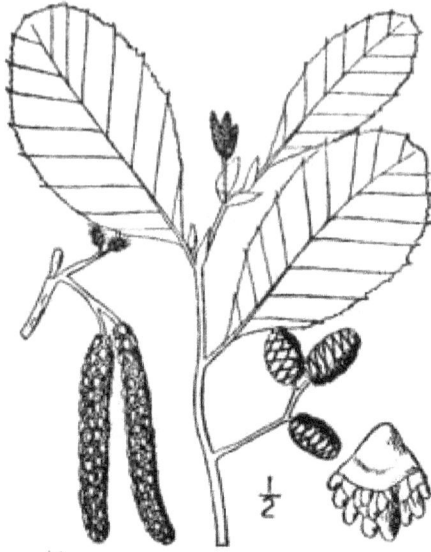

Speckled Alder

The Cycling Seasons

The wind is cold
This late in Autumn….
A chilling touch
Like the morning frost
Which blankets the ground
Creating crystals of ice
Reflecting the sunlight
Shimmering
With their prisms of colour
To dazzle my mind
Their rainbows uplifting
And charming my eyes
Yet within the breeze
Which surrounds me
Its spirals caressing my skin
I feel the Winter storms, their energies
So alive in the sky

I stand here awakened

Refreshed in the knowledge
Of the coming of Spring
Renewal of hope
The lifeblood of all
And with soul felt blessings
I gather the flow
Of the cycling seasons
And drape them upon me
Then smiling release them with the warmth of Summer
To begin yet again
In their constant remembrance
And their bright perseverance
Transformations of time

Ginkgo Biloba

The Dance of Spirals

The dance of spirals turning
Spinning through our lives
Reminders of eternity
Continuing to rise

Within our spirits cyclone
Like eyes of natures' storms
The winds of re-creation
Bring change in all its forms

Eastern Cottonwood

Promise of Destiny

Enfold me in your love
Your drapery of leaves
A cloak to shroud my mysteries
Like mists upon the seas

Then paint me in Earth's colours
In brown and shades of green
With blue my inner eyesight
Like skies' collected dreams

Protect my soul with passion
With orange and fiery red
Your white light coalescing
So wreathed about my head

Through fields of gold I journey
To mountains purple highness
As I seek my lifetimes pathway
My destiny, my promise

Arrowleaf Violet

Forget Me Not

Walking through a forest
With trees of many years
Where green obscures the sunlight
And misty rain appears

I chanced upon a streambed
So covered there with flowers
And stood as if in reverie
As time passed by for hours

Awakened by my senses
By scents, upon the breeze
I gazed about in wonder
Entranced by what I'd seen

A woman there approached me
Dressed in light translucent gown
With faery wings of gossamer
And hair in shades of brown

With eyes of purest lavender
As she peered into my own
Inside my thoughts she showed me
The pathway to her home

For all throughout this woodland
Are many ways, unseen
And only by this memory
Could I return to dream

Before she must now leave me
But only for a while
She kissed me there in silence
And blessed me with her smile

Her voice the sweetest music
This moment never fled
"Forget me not my dreamer"
Were all the words she said.

Halberdleaf Rosemallow

The Vision

She reaches out to others
Gathers them inside
Emerging from their shadows
Out from where they hide

This soul she has a wisdom
A vision that shall shine
Expressions of her spirit
Flowing like a rhyme

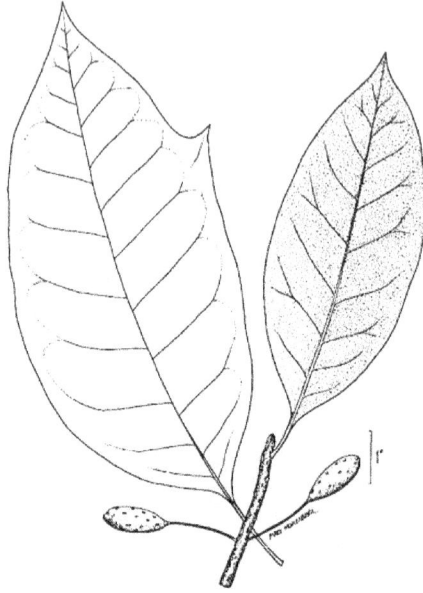

Water Tupelo

Wisdom of the Waves

Standing by the lake
With all its many songs
I meditate in wonder
And feel like I belong

Within the gentle water
The wisdom of the days
While sunlight splashes sweetly
Caressed upon the waves

Sponge Plant

Timeless Whispers

Whispering waters are the calm in the sea
Breathing new life to the dawn

Tossing the waves as they drift from the wind
Chimes mark the start of what's gone

Stars fall at nighttime and gleam off the mist
Mirrored light reflections with a glow

Like a blossoming aurora with a charm about the air
An ecstasy of timeless beauty flow

Trevor L. Schaible

Bamboo

For the Love of the Wind

My fondness, my feelings, my gift to the wind,
For all of those moments I've journeyed within

In dreams I am flying, at one with the sky
Among breezes guiding remembering your sigh

For times I've collected within my own soul
A wisdom, your kindness, your gentleness flows

For even when cyclones and thunderstorms rise
I'll always still love you, your all-knowing eyes.

Stinging Nettle

The Woe of the Warrior

May woe be gone from the warrior's soul
And bind him one, adjoin him whole
Forget the raping of his home
As eagles fly, and bison roam

The drums which sound a thunderous storm
Collecting power as winds now form
The tears descend sad from the skies
To cleanse the Earth before it dies

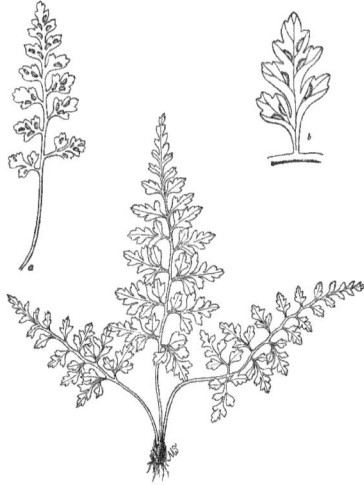

Mountain Spleenwort

The River of Mist

The mist rose from the river
A cloak of mystery
Enshrouded depths with unknown breaths
For nothing can you see

Deepening perceptions
You sense without your eyes
And follow paths of wisdom
For enlightened are the wise

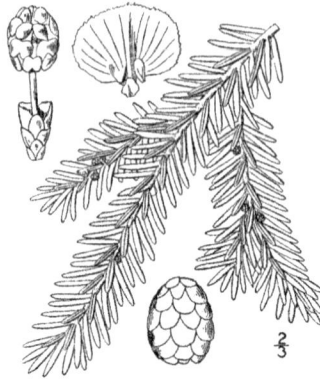

Eastern Hemlock

The Creatures Worth

There is so much beauty
Within your own mind
This soothing remembrance
Of one who is kind

So why must you anger
And torment the Earth
Consuming its creatures
And all they are worth?

Stellaria Media, Chickweed

Sacred Stars

Her starry eyes
Her lovely face
So filled with wonder
And sacred grace

With hope they are lifting
Toward shining skies
Her soul of forever
So blessed as it flies

Wild Indigo

Portrait of a Dawn

A waterfall of sunlight
As seen throughout the mist
Reflected into rainbows
While steady breeze persists

Emotions in the colours
Now shown within the rays
With dazzling bursts of harmony
So mesmerized my gaze

Particles of energy
In quantum fields begun
Creating nature's pictures
With form become as one

The weaving of this pattern
This tapestry of song
Revealing the perfection
Portrayed amidst the dawn

Paper Mulberry

Ode to a Mortal

I am a book with a fading cover
Inside is a tale in which nothing dies
My pages they glow, they want life forever
But the conflict within tries to blind out these eyes

Prophetic words, sung by the seasons
Foretold is the future, to help this mankind
A friendship I weave, a web full of reasons
Suspended in time, this my soul you shall find

Witch Hazel

Life's Mystery

I touch upon the boundaries
My spirit's inner breath
And realize in wonder
At such a greater depth

For while I am seeking
And journeying I see
This timeless path of wisdom
My own life's mystery

Ladies Mantle

Journey from the Unicorn

I travel through these forests
With strength to persevere
So beautiful my journey
With everything so clear

For I have felt her gentle touch
From Earth and from Above
And now return with wisdom
Her sweet embrace of love

My journey there was sacred
Amidst the waterfall
It told of nature's purity
Which rests within us all

The sound it's never distant now
A harmony so near
For always I'll remember
As it never disappears

Trillium

A Breath of Inspiration

So now returns the colours
In many shapes and forms
Awakening the imagery
Of senses now reborn

The verdant shades of Springtime
With Winter chased away
This breath of inspiration
An emotional display

Elm

Infinite Reflections

I see the subtle changes
They happen through your eyes
For every moment gathered
Revealing you are wise

Through all those paths of knowledge
Projections of your past
The endless possibilities
Infinity so vast